BECKY'S GUIDE TO RAISING
Backyard Chickens

Warning	3
Forward	5
In This Book I'll Answer These Questions	6
My Personal Journey With Backyard Chickens	7
Is It Legal In My Area	12
How Long Do Chickens Live?	14
The Coop	15
What Supplies Do I Need To Get Started?	19
What Do Chickens Eat?	21
Where To Buy Chickens	24
Predators	26
How To Keep Your Chickens Healthy In Winter	30
How Can I Tell If My Chicken Is Sick?	34
Chicken Breeds	37
Choosing A Breed	43
Baby Chickens	47
Egg Production	54
My Natural Chicken Dewormer That Really Works	57
Apple Cider Vinegar For Chickens	60
How Long Do Farm Fresh Eggs Last?	61
Roosters	62
Do I Need A Rooster?	67
What Is Broody?	68
How Do Chickens Reproduce?	69
Picking A Good Rooster	71
How To Build A Chicken Coop	73
Cleaning Your Chicken Coop	97
Weird Little Things Chickens Do And Why	99
Ducks	104
Checklists	107
Chicken Breed Index	109

Warning

The information in this book is delivered to you "As Is", without any warranty. While every reasonable effort has been made in writing this book to make sure it's accurate and helpful, errors and omissions can and do occur. This book is not completely comprehensive and you might want to consult other books for advice. This book does not contain professional advice. We won't have any liability to you or anyone else with respect to loss or damage caused or alleged to be caused directly or indirectly in connection with this book.

Forward

I have a great love for chickens. There are so many things to like and enjoy about these funny birds. I get a love of birds from my father and it's so funny how my brothers and sister have the same thing, so it must be in our DNA.

Through my decades of experience raising chickens I've learned the best, healthiest way to house, feed, and keep chickens. I want to share this information with everyone out there who has the desire to raise chickens.

I like to keep all my animals the closest to natural living as possible, I find they're the happiest and healthiest living that way. Nothing is happy when it's too crowded, therefore I give my chickens plenty of living room to thrive in a natural happy way. The benefits are less disease, no need for medication, less stress on the birds…and you. So you have more time to spend enjoying them.

In This Book I'll Answer These Questions

Are chickens legal in my neighborhood?

What supplies do I need to get started?

How big does the coop need to be?

How do I protect my chickens from predators?

What are the best chicken breeds for egg production?

What's the best food for good egg production?

How do I de-worm my chickens naturally?

Will I need a rooster?

How to store my fresh eggs?

How do I care for baby chicks?

My Personal Journey With Backyard Chickens

I finally had a yard. I've always been an animal lover and wherever I lived I would have and enjoy whatever animals that were allowed. Sometimes that was just a cat and a fish aquarium when I lived in a three story walk up. I always wanted more, because I'm so drawn to nature and a natural kind of lifestyle. I feel happiest outside.

As soon as I had my own yard and built a little barn for my horses, the chicken coop was next.

It was slow going because I was very poor, but I didn't care one bit, because I had a big yard. You can get a lot done with very little money, lots of hard work, and a creative imagination.

At first, I didn't care at all about what breed to get. I just wanted chickens and found people nearby that were poor and had way too many horses for their situation, so I bartered some horse feed for a few chickens. One of them was a little half bantam hen I called little mama. She lived to 10 years old and had many, many babies.

The farm fresh eggs have been a staple in my diet ever sense. Through the years I've tried many different breeds and have enjoyed them all. Some breeds do lay a few more eggs than others, but I've found that if you keep them healthy and feed them right they all lay fine. So I just choose the ones I like, and as long as they have plenty of room and don't bully each other it's all good on Becky's Homestead.

What I love about chickens is how playful and happy they are. They seem like they enjoy each and every day pecking around, all sprawled out taking a dust bath or chasing a bug down, chickens seem to do it all with exuberance. I never get tired of watching them or taking care of them.

One thing we learned from experience is that chickens are the ultimate prey bird and everything wants to eat them. We have to be ever vigilant protecting them from predators.

I've learned through the years not to hate the predators, I never blame them, I blame myself for not building a safe enough coop, and for not having a good farm dog on duty. I don't hate the fox for being a fox. I don't hate the owl for being an owl. I blame myself for not protecting my chickens and doing what I should have.

That's why I always, always tell people who want chickens to first build a good strong coop, then go get the chickens. It is super tempting and exciting when you are in a store or at a flea market that sells chickens, to just get a few and 'while they grow' you will get some kind of coop built. That's not a good idea. Nobody does good work while under pressure with a deadline looming. That pressure is even worst when it comes to animal housing. The pressure feels unbearable while you're looking at those chickens growing bigger and bigger every day and you need to get them in a coop.

That's when the shortcut seems like it will be ok 'just for now' and Mr. Fox is waiting on the sidelines licking his lips. Just believe me, and build a good coop first then bring home the chicks. You will save yourself a lot of trouble.

In this book I touch on many things I have learned and hope that my experience will help you enjoy your chickens as much as I enjoy mine and keep them happy and healthy.

Raising Chickens For Beginners

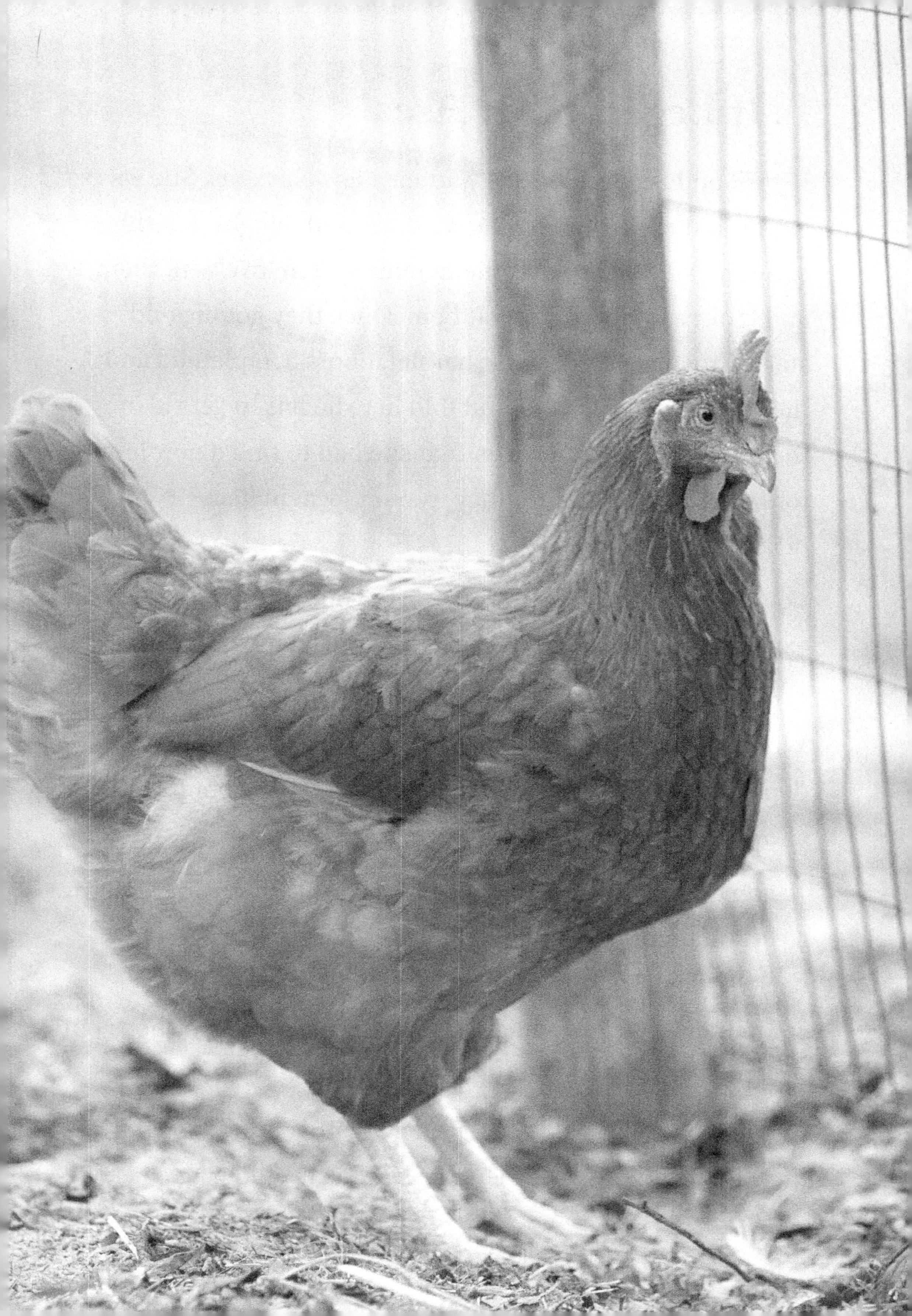

Is It Legal In My Area

My friend Lisa decided she wanted a few chickens. She was so happy and excited when she went out and bought 4 darling baby chicks. She brought them home, fell in love with them, and took really good care of them. Once they got big and started to make some noise her neighbors complained and the authorities came out and told her she has to get rid of them. She was heart broken that she had to find a new home for her chickens because they weren't legal in her neighborhood.

To make sure this doesn't happen to you, I'm going to explain exactly how to find out if chickens are legal in your neighborhood. It's very simple to check.

What you do is call the town hall, ask for the zoning department, give them your address, and ask them if you're allowed to have chickens.

In some towns they've passed a special rule that you can have a certain number of chickens in a residential area because backyard chickens are so popular now. For example sometimes your town might say, 'You can have three hens but no roosters.'

In some places people have gotten together and lobbied the local authorities to pass new rules officially allowing chickens.

So even if chickens aren't currently allowed where you live it's not hopeless.

Thankfully Lisa found a good home for her chickens, they now live on a farm in the country.

How Long Do Chickens Live?

Before I get started on a project I like to know what I'm getting myself into - what kind of commitment am I really making? It's hard to plan for a pet when you don't know how long it lives. You need to know what's involved in the project. Is it a two year project or a ten year project? Some people might be willing to commit to a two year project, but if it's ten years they might be like 'whoa, thats too much. It's good to know what you're getting into.

Chickens live about four to ten years. I had one live ten years befour. I would say chickens are a long term commitment if you take good care of them, which I'm going to show you how to do in this book ;)

I love raising chickens because they're so much fun to watch and they give me fresh tasty eggs. In my opinion they're easier to take care of than a cat or a dog, plus they're cute and they each have their own personality.

The Coop

Joan was browsing around the flea market.

She excitedly bought three adult hens and brought them home without any supplies.

She has a little farm, so she thought she could manage, and they would be happy there free ranging. when night came the chickens didn't have anywhere to sleep, so as all chickens do, they jumped up in a tree to roost, and around 1am she heard an awful noise. Bye bye chicken. She quickly realized her new chickens need a coop. What I recommend is building the coop first, then go shopping for chickens.

There are two parts to a chicken coop.

There's the wooden wind proof, weather proof part called the hen house. Your hens will sleep and lay eggs in the hen house. They will sleep on a roost and lay their eggs in a nest box.

Attached to the hen house is the chicken run, it's made of wire and it's like a fenced in exercise yard where they go out and get fresh air and sunshine. They love to scratch around in the run and also take a nice dust bath in the sand.

These two parts together equal the chicken coop.

You need to have the right size chicken coop for the number of hens you have. It's critical for their health.

How much room do my chickens need?

Each chicken needs twenty five square feet of room in the coop. That works out to be a five foot by five foot area for each chicken. This gives them plenty of room to grow and live a healthy life. Over crowding is the number one mistake people make and it leads to a lot of health problems.

Poor health and stress equals low egg production. You'll get way more eggs from two happy hens than you will from 10 overcrowded sick hens, and remember those sick hens will still be costing you money for feed with nothing in return.

My wooden hen house is eight by eight feet square and seven feet high so I can stand in there.

The run is eight by sixteen feet long

So the coop is eight by twenty four foot long total.

The wooden hen house is one third of the total size of the coop.

I keep eight hens in there year round.

I recommend building the hen house out of wood. It has to be weatherproof, wind proof, and predator proof. So wood is a really good way to go, it's a bit of a project but it's well worth it.

Joan learned the hard way that you need a chicken coop to protect your chickens and keep them alive, because there are predators lurking around looking for the opportunity to eat your chickens. That's called nature. And you don't fight nature, you out smart nature. Joan watched some of my videos about building a chicken coop and she emailed me to let me know that now she has a sturdy chicken coop filled with happy safe chickens. Now we can all sleep safe at night.

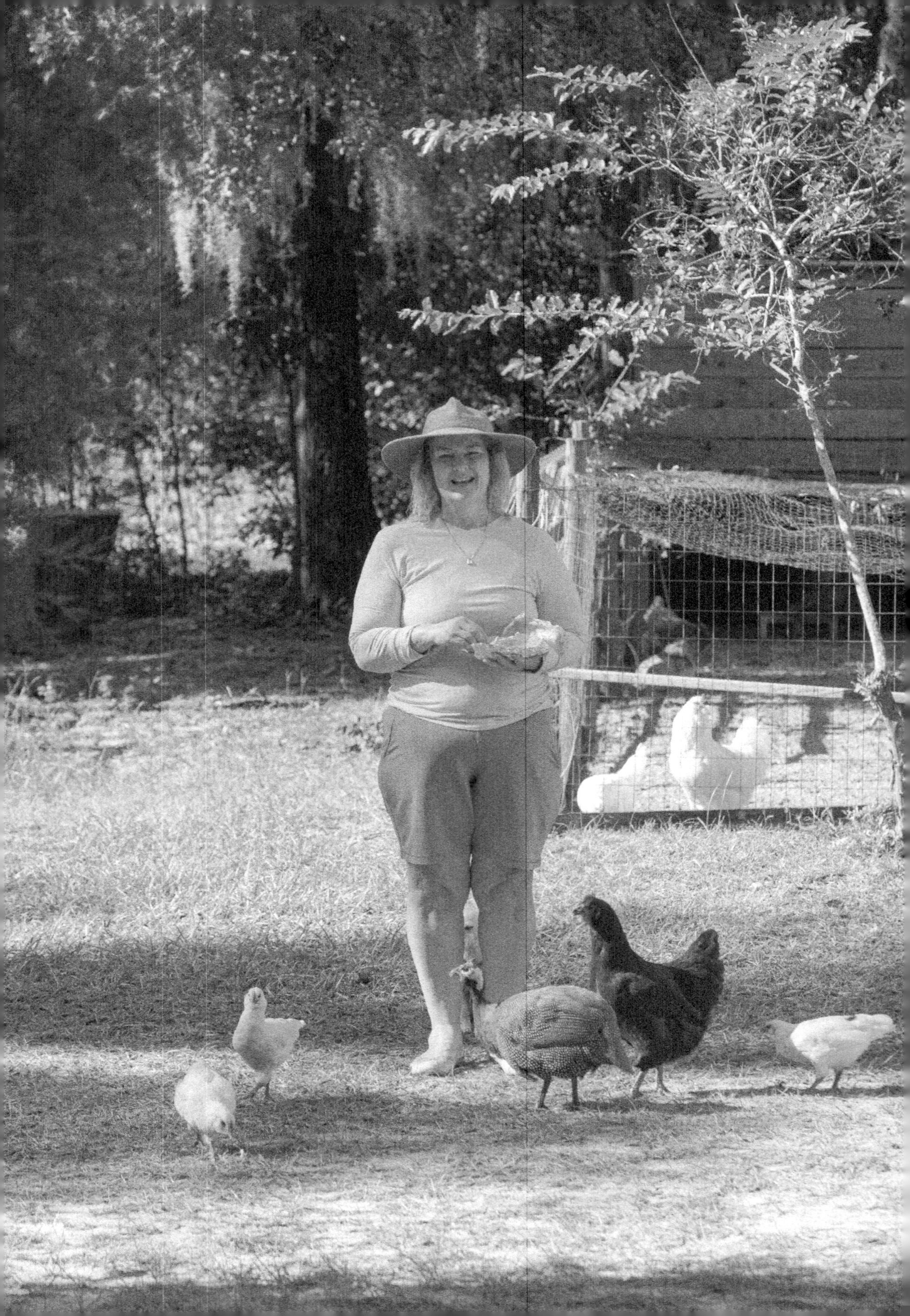

What Supplies Do I Need To Get Started?

I have a shallow rubber water tub in my chicken coop that I've used for years. I love it and most importantly the chickens love it. I also have a hanging automatic chicken feeder which is super handy, especially when I go away. It makes the job easier for my pet sitter, which is always a good thing.

Another thing you need in your hen house is a nesting box, this is where they lay their eggs. I have a video showing you how to make an easy inexpensive nest box.

I use a tuff stuff food barrel to keep chicken food in, I keep that in my barn. It makes it super handy and the food never gets moldy, wet, and bugs can't get in it. It keeps the food really fresh. Fresh clean food keeps your chickens healthy.

I buy a 10 pound bag of Diatomaceous Earth (DE) on amazon and l keep it in a giant animal cracker tub from Sam's Club. (Animal crackers are a great treat for all my animals, they all love them.) I use the DE to de-worm my chickens, I'll talk about that more in a later chapter.

I buy a 50 lb bag of crushed oyster shells. The chickens eat this for grit, it helps them digest their food and gives them calcium so they're egg shells are hard. Your chickens have to have grit on a daily basis. It comes in a sturdy bag and I just keep that in my barn. Hens absolutely have to have calcium for two reasons. Number one, for strong shells and number two, for strong muscles to push out their eggs so they don't get egg bound.

What Do Chickens Eat?

What do chickens eat? That is a very common question from new owners and some long time owners as well.

The reason is everyone wants beautiful healthy chickens that lay a lot of eggs. Most chickens lay pretty steady for the first year, even if you don't know what your doing. It's after that when the trouble starts. They don't look to good, they stop laying eggs, they get sick and they fight and peck each other.

This leaves everyone thinking What Happened? What am I doing wrong?

Chickens are just like people, if you want to be healthy you have to eat healthy and give your body what it needs. That doesn't mean, give your body what tastes good or what the popular diet of the minute says to eat. What I mean, is feed your chickens what they need to be healthy and productive.

First we have to think about how a loose chicken acts. Is it grazing on grass like a horse or is it scratching in the dirt to find bugs and worms, or does it do both? We can all see for ourselves if we let our chickens loose and sit and watch them. You will get a better idea if you live in the country as apposed to a small yard, but I can tell you they spend more time in the woods looking for bugs than they do eating grass in the yard. In fact when they are in the grass they are looking for seeds and grasshoppers and crickets not eating much grass at all.

I always try and feed all my animals as close to natural as I can. I feed my horses different grass hays because that is what wild horses eat. Why would I change that? Just because feed companies say, 'feed this, it's a balanced diet', and sell a bag of wheat middlings and soybean hulls coated in sugar with some vitamins added, doesn't mean it's a whole food natural diet.

I want to feed myself and all my animals whole food. Yes, a bag of chicken pellets or crumbles can be used but always after, or in addition to all the whole food they want.

I don't even buy pellets or crumbles anymore because my chickens don't eat it and it just goes to waste. They are full and satisfied on their healthy food.

What I Feed My Chickens

Oats, whole corn, black sunflower seeds, meat such as meal worms, table scraps, canned tuna, sardines, high quality canned cat and dog food, and zero grain cat kibble. I also feed some bread for a treat. From my cupboard, I will feed raw oatmeal, crackers, cooked rice or pasta, and fruit and vegetables

I will also feed alfalfa hay. Chickens love alfalfa and it adds calcium as well.

What I Feed Baby Chicks

If mama hen hatches out her own babies, she will take care of them herself. Just make sure you use shallow water bowls like pie plates for their water, so the chicks don't drown. I use two, one at each end of the coop.

If you bought your chicks from a store, buy a bag of non medicated organic chick starter, and a bag of chick grit.

Grit

Every chicken on the planet needs grit from day one to digest their food, so make sure they have it available at all times. I use crushed oyster shells once they have feathers because not only does it act as grit but it also adds calcium to their diet. Hens need calcium for their muscles to work properly so they can push out an egg. Egg bound hens are lacking calcium. you can give them crushed granite grit in addition to the crushed oyster shell if you want to. I feed both.

De-worming

It's very important and can't be stated enough that chickens need to be dewormed on a regular schedule. I use fresh water food grade Diatomaceous Earth and mix it right into their tub of food. I have found over the years that's the easiest way to do it. I mix one cup of DE into 50 pounds of chicken food every time I refill the tub with fresh food.

Where To Buy Chickens

It's a good idea to buy your chickens from a well known store. Especially if you want pure breed chickens. That way you know exactly what you're getting. I like Tractor Supply for online ordering because, they have free shipping. They have a lot of breeds to choose from year round with that free shipping, that gives them the edge in my opinion. Some hatcheries have a great price on the birds, and then it's $35 for the shipping. That's kind of a deal breaker for me. Unless it's a very specific fancy breed I can't find anywhere else, then it's worth it I'll pay the money for shipping. Here are a couple online hatcheries I've bought from in the past;

- Tractor Supply
- Meyer Hatchery

Most local feed stores carry chickens in the spring, it's just a thing they all do. When I go to buy chickens I want hens for the farm fresh eggs. I don't want to buy a bunch of babies and end up with 4 roosters and 2 hens, which could happen if you don't know the chicken terminology.

What is a pullet?

Pullets are hens, females, baby girls.

What does straight run mean?

Straight run is mixed males and females. Girls and boys mixed in the same tub or cage, you don't know what your getting.

What is a cockerel?

Cockerels are roosters, males, boy chickens.

Remember these terms when you're ordering so you get what you want. You pick out the breed you want and the sex you want. A lot of hatcheries and stores make the straight run cheaper. Don't be tempted by the low prices because getting several roosters from the straight run is a pain in the neck down the road. Always buy pullets which are hens - females - for your backyard coop.

Predators

Here are some predators that like to eat chickens

- Possums
- Raccoons
- Foxes
- Dogs
- some Cats
- Coyotes
- Wild Pigs
- Hawks and some owls

I want to take a second here to say, never hate nature. It is your job to supply a safe coop for your chickens. That is the part you can control. You will never have to worry about the predators if you build a good sturdy coop.

Pretty much all animals are above a chicken and can eat it. That's why they invented chicken coops, because the odds are stacked against a loose chicken. Chickens have no defenses and they are not that smart. The stress of being so vulnerable makes a loose chicken useless, it's going to be so nervous it won't lay many eggs, it won't keep much weight on, and it will be super flighty.

Now that I've covered what's after your chicken, which is pretty much everything, I'll talk about some ways to predator proof your chicken coop, and harden the target.

The best and most important thing I do to protect my chickens is build a good sturdy chicken coop. I invest all my money and time building a really strong coop, and that means a wooden hen house, and a wire chicken run.

The wire I use for the chicken run is really strong. Picture in your mind a big fat forty pound raccoon standing on the top of your wire run. I don't want the wire to sag, bend, or break. I want a very sturdy chicken run that's going to hold up to lurking predators.

Some people might live way in the country and have more predators than someone in the suburbs or in town. For the people that live way out in the country and have more predators around it might be a good idea to have a wire floor on the chicken run. So nothing can dig under the edge and get in there. What I do to keep my chickens happy and healthy is I dump sand over the wire floor so they can still get their dust bath. Also no matter where you live, having a sand floor in the chicken run is awesome. It's easy to clean and has great drainage. To keep the sand in there I put pressure treated two by sixes around the edge and nail them on the outside of the run so it's like a sandbox that keeps the sand inside and it doesn't wash way.

My hen house is built out of four by four corner posts, with wood farm boards on all four sides and a tin roof. The door is a nice little door I made myself out of the same boards, with some metal hinges and a hook and loop closure. The roof is made of tin and has stood up to many severe Florida storms.

Building my hen house out of wooden boards is just the best thing I ever did. It's big and shady, rain proof and blocks noise. The hens spend a lot of time in there and feel safe and comfortable. They go right in to lay their eggs, and go right in at night to roost, they feel secure and happy in their wooden henhouse.

If anyone feels like they need a second line of defense, because of having an issue with predators. A strand or two of electric fence will do the trick. How you install electric fence is you put the first strand 6 inches above the ground all the way around the coop. Then a 2nd strand 12 inches above the ground. One nice thing about using the electric fence nowadays is they make a solar charger box so you don't need to run an extension cord out to the coop.

My third line of defense is a good farm dog. I've always had one to help protect my chickens. What they do is scare off the predators. A dog is very useful because they're on guard 24/7. I treat mine right and they become very protective of my homestead.

How To Keep Your Chickens Healthy In Winter

If your chickens don't have a way to get out of the weather and aren't fed the correct food they might not make it through the winter or might struggle in the extreme cold.

If you do these few things they will be happy and healthy all winter long.

First and foremost is the henhouse. Make double, triple sure it's completely wind, rain, and snow proof.

When animals are able to stay out of the wind and stay dry the battle is almost won. It's when they get wet or the cold wind blows on them that they can struggle and even die.

After the henhouse is completely weather proofed for the winter we need to add a thick layer of wood chips on the floor. Don't be skimpy, six to eight inches is about right. You can buy bags of compressed "horse bedding" really cheap at Tractor Supply Co. and other feed stores. While you're at the feed store also buy a bale of alfalfa hay. Throw the whole bale of hay on top of the wood chips. They need the green food and it smells awesome. The chickens will love it.

The next thing we have to do is feed them a lot of animal protein. Well fed animals grow in a nice thick winter coat, for some that means extra fur and for chickens it means extra downy feathers.

What I mean by animal protein is meat like tuna fish, sardines, canned cat or dog food. I try and buy organic if I can swing it. High quality "no grain added" cat kibble works well too. Black oil sunflower seeds are a great thing to add as well. Whole corn is awesome because it's high in fat and is a staple around here.

Also crushed oyster shells as grit is a must to make sure they grind up all their food and the calcium keeps their egg laying muscles in good working order. We don't want any egg bound hens in our coop. Just like us they need extra calories during the winter when it's cold outside. I'm extra hungry when it's cold.

Another thing you can do is make sure one roost is wider so when they squat down to sleep at night their body feathers cover their toes and keeps them warm. We all know cold feet are miserable. I make one roost about three inches in diameter and one a bit wider.

If for some reason you notice a chicken not doing well, I would pull that one out and maybe keep it in the garage in a small cage with a heat lamp. Don't keep it too warm or you'll not be able to put it back outside. It can't go from warm to cold just like that. When it's better you will have to wait until a sunny warmer day, then put it back.

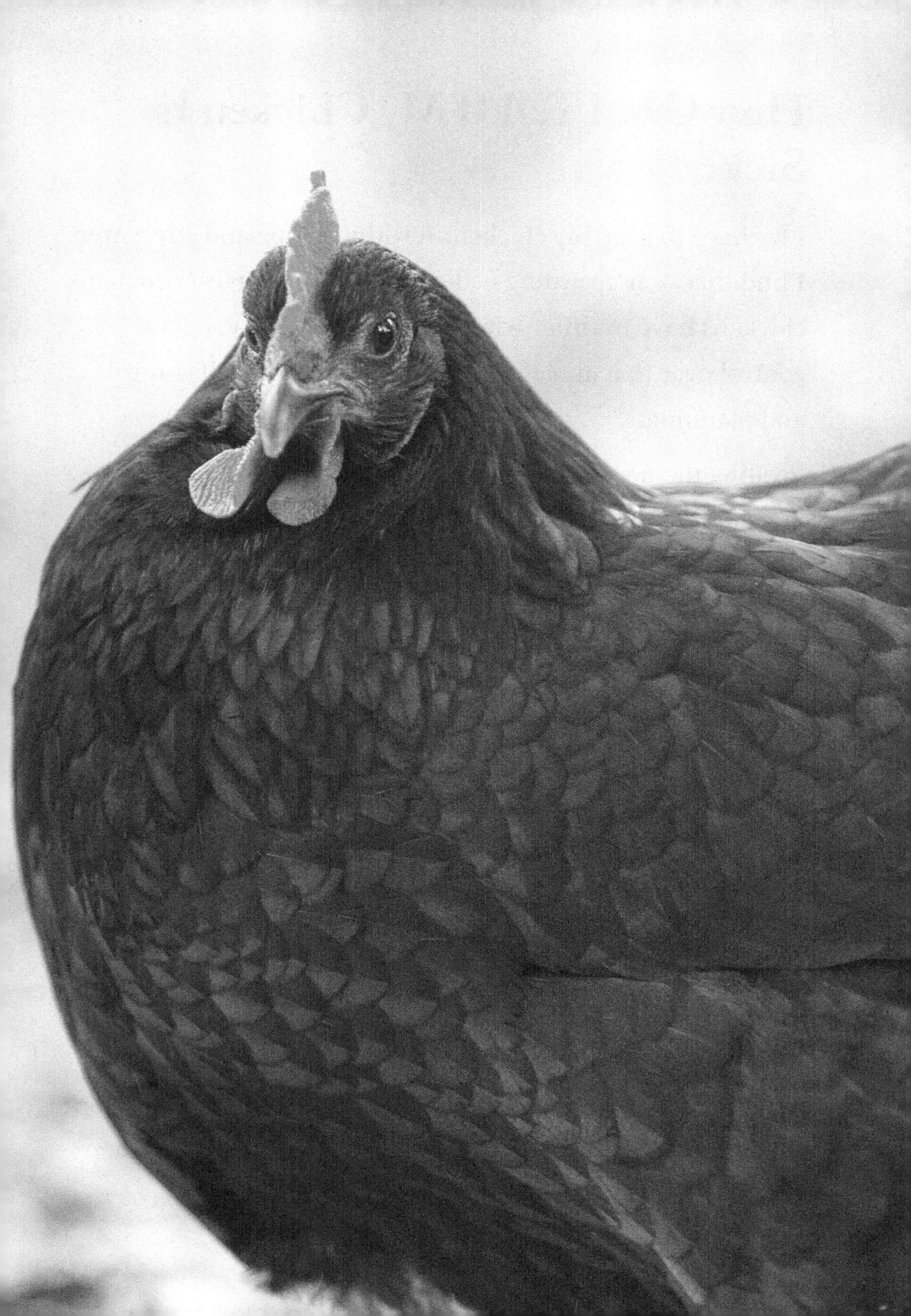

How Can I Tell If My Chicken Is Sick?

I try hard to keep my chickens healthy, happy and stress free. I find that over crowding is the number one biggest problem chickens have to suffer with. The good thing is you have control over that and can prevent it with some self control and planning.

Feeding them everything they need to stay healthy is a huge, huge part of preventing diseases. As with any living thing on the planet, prevention is way better than treating the disease, but from time to time it happens so here are the three most common diseases.

The first two are very treatable if you catch them early and isolate the chicken, so always have a wire cage for emergencies.

1) Fowl Pox Virus

What you need to know about Fowl Pox is there are two types. One type is more mild and the chicken gets over it in about three weeks. What you will see are Pox on the red part of their head and "chin" which are called the waddle and comb. You might also see some on their beaks. Isolate the chicken, keep them warm but not hot, never hot. Put a teaspoon of apple cider vinegar in their water. One teaspoon in two cups of water. Feed as normal and keep them clean and quiet. After three weeks you can put them back in the coop if all the Pox are completely gone.

The second type is much worse and it's a good chance the chicken will die. That is because it seems they inhale the virus so the pox develop in their mouth and down their throat. If yours have this type you can cull them or isolate them and try and treat them and see what happens.

2) Infectious Bronchitis Virus

The first thing you need to know about Infectious Bronchitis is it is very, very contagious. Quickly isolate sick birds and disinfect your whole coop once a week for a month. You can use 1 gallon of white vinegar and one gallon of water mixed together then pour it in a large spray bottle. Spray everything, nest boxes, roost, floor, the whole outside run, everything.

The signs of Infectious Bronchitis are the chicken will be gasping for air, and mucus will be running from it's nose and beak. It's feathers will look ruffled and it will be coughing or sneezing. It will be crouching in a corner trying to keep warm. Put the chicken in a wire cage out of the wind and put a heat lamp on it to keep it warm, not hot, never hot, just nice and cozy and quiet. Put a teaspoon of apple cider vinegar in two cups of water for it to drink. Feed it normal and see how it goes. I will feed a little wet bread, dipped in the vinegar and water, they seem to like that.

3) Mareks Disease Virus

Mareks Disease is another virus. Pull any sick looking chicken out of your coop fast, because viruses spread fast and step one is damage control. The signs you will see in your chicken are paralyzed legs or wings. Sometimes it will be one leg and one wing. If your chicken gets Mareks Disease it will die, so just make it as comfortable as you can or cull it.

All three of these viruses attack young and weak chickens. Put all your time and money into feeding the best diet you can, and make double triple sure your coop is not over crowded. Keep their water clean, and giving your chicken coop a good scrub down every six months will also help reduce disease.

Chicken Breeds

Types Of Chickens

We put chickens into three types according to what they are good at.

- Meat birds also called broilers are bred for meat.
- Egg layers are for lots of eggs.
- Dual purpose breeds are good at both laying eggs and broiling.

It's good to think about what you want and need your chickens for before you go chicken shopping.

Of course you can eat breeds that are classified as egg layers and you could use broilers as egg layers, but to keep your flock as efficient as possible to save money and get a good product it's smart to know your chicken types.

You can also get mixed breeds such as a Barred Rock hen and a Leghorn rooster that make babies together like on my homestead. I love my chickens and they become what I like to call "working pets". They have a job to do around here, but I love them.

If you're on a tight budget or are only allowed a few hens, it really pays to get the right type so you get the most for all your time and effort.

Best Egg Laying Chickens

Some people choose a breed for the amount of eggs they can expect to get, but if you take good care of your chickens and do everything right, you'll get steady egg production from any breed. All chickens lay eggs and any chicken that is well fed and happy and healthy will lay better than a chicken that is not well fed, wormy, and stressed out in an overcrowded coop. Half the fun of keeping chickens is picking out ones that are appealing to you – be it color, cuteness or whatever.

These breeds have proven over the years to be exceptional egg layers.

White Leghorn

They lay white eggs, all the commercial egg farmers use this breed because they eat the least amount of feed and lay the most eggs. So they're an economical egg layer.

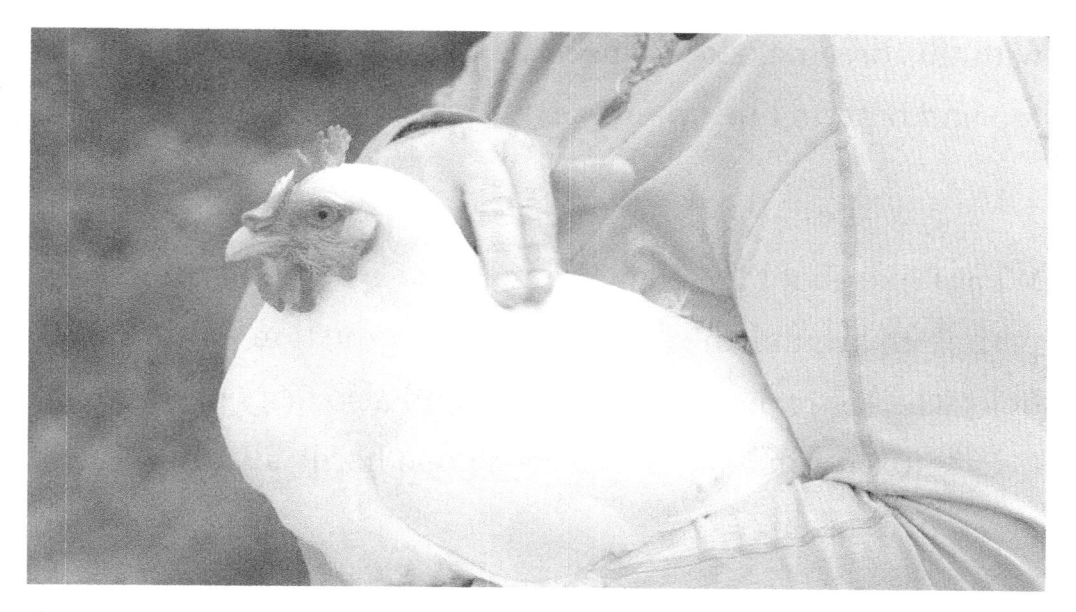

Ameraucana

I've owned Ameraucans for years, I love this breed because they're independent and feisty.

Plus they lay greenish eggs. (only the shell is greenish, the inside is normal). When you pick out the babies make sure they don't have a crossed beak, that's a common problem with this breed. So look closely at the beak and make sure the top and bottom line up properly.

New Hampshire Red

What I like about the New Hampshire Red breed is they are a perfect all around chicken. Good egg production – broody hens which equals good mothers – and also tasty meat if you decide to eat some of them. Just a good hardy all around breed of chicken.

Black Australorp

Black Australorps are a super friendly breed. If you're a little afraid of chickens to start with you can't go wrong with these.

Just keep in mind that if you decide to add more chickens to your flock down the road that Black Australorps can be bullies to other chickens. Which is kind of funny that they are people friendly but chicken bullies.

Broiler or Meat Birds

Cornish

Cornish are probably the best meat bird but they grow so fast and get so heavy they can not take the heat very well at all. For that reason take extra care while raising them.

Brahma's are a great meat bird because of their size. Roosters are 12 pounds and hens about 9 pounds. Brahma's are gentle giants.

Cochin

Cochins are like The Cornish in that they do not handle the heat well at all, so be careful.

Dual Purpose Breeds

I chose these three breeds because in my opinion they have all the good qualities for homesteaders. They are both heat and cold hardy. They all lay large to medium eggs and they are all broody breeds (broody is when a hen sits on the eggs to try and hatch them). Of course you can either eat them or have them for eggs or both.

- Jersey Giant

- Orpington
- New Hampshire

Choosing A Breed

Choosing a chicken breed to get for your flock is so exciting because there are so many different kinds of chickens. Different sizes, different colors, different temperaments, and different colored eggs. There are different breeds for different purposes, but I'm going to focus on egg layers in this book.

The first thing you have to think about when choosing a breed is the climate where you live. There are cold hardy breeds, and breeds that do better in the heat.

Cold Hardy Chicken Breeds

Any chicken breed with furry feet is a good choice for cold weather as well as any heavy breed.

- Chochin (come in a variety of colors)
- Brahmas
- Buff Orpington
- New Hampshire Reds

Hot Weather Breeds

All chickens need dark dark shade in the summer, with a big pan of water also in the shade. I recommend building your hen house in dark shade under a tree and then the run can project out into the sunlight. That way in the summer your chickens have a choice of dark shade or sunlight.

- Black Australorp
- Red or Black Sex Link
- Ameraucana

Pretty Chickens
Buff Orpington

They're a big poofy golden chicken, they're so beautiful, I love buff orpingtons.

They're very friendly and docile so they can get picked on if you have them mixed with other breeds. A lot of people will just have buff orpingtons alone to prevent them from getting picked on.

Quiet Chicken Breeds

Chickens are so much fun and fresh eggs are delicious and healthy. A lot more people would love to give raising a couple hens a try but fear they are noisy and that neighbors will start complaining, and the joy will soon turn into misery.

If you don't have a big yard and your neighbors are close, you can still raise a couple hens with success. Placing your coop in the right place in the yard and choosing the right breed of hen will get you off to a good start.

Another thing that will help keep the coop quiet is to choose two or three of the same breed of hen. It seems to me that the same kind of chickens stick together, thus the old saying "birds of a feather, flock together". This will help make sure that everyone gets along and no one will be the odd hen out, because that will cause stress and stress will cause commotion and commotion equals noise.

The breed of hen that I love the most for several reasons is the Black Australorp. They are quiet and so sweet. They are heat and cold hardy, they lay large brown eggs and they lay lots of them.

The hens are also broody, which means they will sit and hatch their own chicks if you have a rooster. So for me they are my number one choice.

My second choice is the Buff Orpington, these hens are sweet and friendly like the Black Australorps. They are slightly bigger, usually around seven pounds but their beautiful fluffy gold feathers make them look huge. They can't handle hot weather, so you must make double sure your hen house is under a tree in dark shade.

They handle the cold much better than the heat. They are broody and will also sit and hatch out their own chicks if you have a rooster just like the Black Australorp's.

I have personally owned both these breeds and love them so much, that is why I recommend them to anyone who wants to give backyard chickens a try for the first time.

Baby Chickens

Caring For Baby Chicks

When you get your chicky babies home you have to get them all set up.

You will need a tub, heat lamp, bedding, waterer, and a little feeder. Make sure the heat lamp is only on one side of the tub so the chicks have a warm side and a cool side. It's good to have a thermometer because your chicks need to be

ninety five degrees for the first two weeks and then lower the heat five degrees every seven days. Be sure and put some baby chick grit in with the food. They are pretty easy to take care of at this age. Just keep the bedding, food and water clean and lower the heat five degrees every seven days. Always be very gentle when handling the little chicks. Their little legs and wings can get hurt and then they will be damaged for life.

What Do Baby Chicks Eat

I start all my baby chicks out on non medicated chick starter. When I can get non-medicated and organic chick starter I get that. All baby chicks need grit right from the get go. They make very finely crushed grit specifically for little tiny chicks. Make sure you get a bag of that. I put a little in their food every day, this makes the chicks grow really beautiful and healthy. At about 2 months old I start offering crimped oats, alfalfa hay, and meal worms. At this age I also let them have outside time so they can eat some grass and pick around for some bugs themselves.

When To Give Chickens Grit

Giving your chickens grit at all times is very important. It prevents a lot of problems from even getting started. Grit is so crucial for the chickens digestive system that a lack of grit can cause a backup and then the chicken will develop sour crop. Sour crop is when the food gets backed up and clogged and then a yeast infection starts inside the chicken's crop. Your best line of defense is preventing all these little things from happening in the first place by giving your baby chicks grit from day one. They make grit especially for baby chicks called "chick grit". They have to have it 24/7. when they get older, about four months of age I add crushed oyster shells.

When Do Chickens Get Feathers?

When chickens hatch from the egg they have adorable little chicky fuzz. They immediately start growing their feathers, it happens right away! I always notice the little wing feathers grow in first, the body feathers come in next, then the head and neck feathers grow in last. They'll be fully feathered in about 2 months, you won't see any chicky fuzz, it will all be covered and they'll look like mini chickens. Once they grow up chickens have fuzzy down on the inside, and regular feathers on the outside. The fuzzy down is what keeps them warm and that part grows in thicker in the winter. Even though you can't see the fuzzy down, it's like a winter coat under there.

When To Put Baby Chicks In The Coop?

Pretty soon your chicks will be too big for the tub, but too small for the coop. The biggest dilemma about the baby chicks at this age is their size. They're bigger now and much more active, they need more room to grow and be healthy. They look capable but they're still very vulnerable because of their small size. They are fully feathered like adult chickens, only smaller. At this age they still need special care. That's why I'm going to move them to a small private chicken coop to give them more time to grow, and be protected from aggressive adult chickens until they are big enough to defend themselves.

Leaving them in the tub too long creates a lot of stress. They reach a certain size where they have a lot of energy and they need more room to release that energy. If they stay cramped in the baby tub they will start picking on each other and for sure the weakest one will get bullied. At this time the tub is too small and cramped and it will be dirty and stinky unless you clean it every other day. And that starts to be more trouble than it's worth, and it's just much more convenient to move them into a bigger coop.

If I put them in the big coop with the adults now it's practically certain death. For whatever reason the hens don't accept them into the flock at this size. Once they're the same size as the adult chickens they will be accepted into the flock. To avoid any problems and headaches I just put them in their own coop and give them time to grow. Running a homestead is much more enjoyable and peaceful when you avoid problems. Having a small transitional coop is very easy and well worth it. It's not a waste of money to invest in a small transitional coop because it's useful throughout the year for other things like; a sick chicken or duck, a small dog, a baby pig. You could even put plants in there to keep them safe. You can also use it as a chicken coop for 2 adult chickens. I show you how to build this simple practical coop step-by-step later in this book.

How To Introduce New Chickens To A Flock

Once the babies are about the same size as adults chickens, around four months old. It's time to put them in the adult chicken coop with the others. If you are adding babies to the coop with adults you will have to make a couple adjustments. You will need two feeders and two water pans. Put a food bowl and a water pan on each end of the coop. This will make sure the young chickens always have access to food and water during the "getting to know you" phase. Chickens have a pecking order and when you add new ones there is a crazy period where they kind of chase and peck each other a bit. Keep an eye on them to make sure things are going good and everyone is eating and drinking. Things should settle down in a couple weeks. As far as the nest boxes go, one nest box for every eight hens is good. A lot of times they seem to all love one, but I just like to make sure they have enough just in case.

Egg Production

How To Get Good Egg Production

Step one, The Nest Box

This is where she is going to go to lay her egg, so it's very important. People don't give enough thought to the nest box. Here are the key components to a good nest box. It has to be in a private corner in the hen house. They're not going to lay an egg in the blazing sun. I find that hay is the best nest box bedding. I never put my nest boxes over 2 feet above the ground. Older hens like them even lower than that, for easy access.

Step Two, Peace & Quiet

If the kids are going in and out of the coop all day that's too much activity and that will affect your egg production. I go into my coop in the morning and once in the evening. A pet dog can also be a big disruption, if it's running around the coop barking at the hens it will hurt your egg production. From the hens point of view it's danger danger red alert, they can't relax after that. I treat my hens like pampered little queens. They're nice and relaxed and I have great egg production all the time.

Step Three, Food

It takes a lot of extra calories to lay eggs consistently. It's up to me to provide healthy food for them and I take it very seriously.

The first thing is crushed oyster shells for grit and calcium. If they don't have the grit they can't digest food and without the calcium their egg shells will be soft, they also need the calcium so their muscles can contract and push out the egg, without it they can get egg bound and die. I give them crushed oyster shells because it takes care of all of that.

The seconed thing is they need enough animal protein. Some of the protein they can get themselves from finding bugs, worms, and toads. Since mine live in a coop I have to supplement their animal protein. I haven't found any commercial feed with enough animal protein in it, so I add meal worms, tuna fish, and any meat scraps from the house. Chickens need a lot of animal protein every day. Also high quality grain free cat kibble made with fish or lamb is also really good and they love it. Third is whole corn, because it has the corn oil. Whole corn has the germ which contains the corn oil. Cracked corn doesn't have any oil because the germ has been removed. What I want is the oil for the fat in there diet. Chickens love whole corn and will gobble it right up. When they're young I start with just a handful. I give them a chance to experiment and they all learn to eat it.

Forth is a commercial egg laying crumble. That's just so they can have a variety. I always buy non medicated and organic if I can.

fifth is oats. They love them! Really any kind of oats, crimped oats, oat meal, steamed oats they're all good for hens. I like oats for animal feed, I think it works well and they all like it. After the baby crumbles oats are the first thing my chicks start eating.

I keep the commercial egg laying crumble in the chicken feeder and everything else I scatter in the run every day so they can pick around.

My Natural Chicken Dewormer That Really Works

When you go to collect your eggs is there poop on them? There shouldn't be. Are you thinking "what's this all about"? "What's going on here"? It doesn't seem like there should be poop on the eggs. Are everyone's eggs like this?

No, not everyone's eggs are poopy. When chickens have poopy egg shells it means they need to be dewormed. Chickens only have one "hole" and it's called a vent. Everything comes out that one hole including your eggs, so it's very important to keep your chickens as healthy as possible. Deworming your chickens regularly is a very important step to keeping them healthy.

There's a lot of chemical dewormers out there. I personally try to steer away from as many chemicals as I can. That's why I love and have used diatomaceous earth (DE) for years and years to de-worm all my animals on my homestead, including my chickens! I love this stuff, it's economical, safe and easy to use, and very effective. It's very very important to deworm all your animals at the same time. The indoor and outdoor pets all together. You can't spot de-worm your animals, meaning you de-worm the dog this month, the cat next month, the chickens three months later. That's not an effective way to control internal parasites. De-worming properly not only keeps all your animals happy and healthy, it also saves you money on animal feed. I think worms are the first step in bad health for animals. If you do nothing else for them keeping them de-wormed will increase their lifespan.

How I De-Worm My Chickens With DE

I have found over the years the easiest way to do it is to mix the DE right into the food. That way when I feed they're getting de-wormed a little bit every day. If they already have a worm load it slowly kills them and their body breaks them down and eliminates them.

The mixing ratio I use is one teaspoon of DE per pound of food. That works out to be 1.2 cups per fifty pound bag of feed. So I just do one cup per fifty pound bag, that's how I measure it out. Those are my ratios that have been very effective for me. This ratio works for every animal on my homestead. I use high quality fresh water food grade DE only, you can buy the same kind I use on Amazon.

Apple Cider Vinegar For Chickens

Most chicken viruses and sicknesses spread through their water. overcrowding makes the water dirtier and makes sickness spread faster from chicken to chicken.

It's very important to keep the water super clean. That's why I use a big rubber tub, it holds three gallons of water, and it's super easy to clean. After I clean it I dump in about one fourth cup of apple cider vinegar.

What the apple cider vinegar does is help keep the amount of bacteria down in my water tub.

If your chickens are having a problem with sour crop add more grit and make sure you put apple cider vinegar in their water.

Don't put too much, no one wants to drink pure vinegar, so make sure you measure. I only put 1 tablespoon per gallon.

How Long Do Farm Fresh Eggs Last?

How long do farm fresh eggs last and how do I store them? I collect my eggs daily, I take my egg basket out to the coop, and collect my eggs. I look over the eggs carefully and make sure none of them are cracked. If I find a cracked egg I feed it to my dogs. It's very important to only store undamaged eggs.

I keep my farm fresh eggs on the counter for up to 1 week. We eat a lot of eggs so they don't stay around here long because they're so delicious. If I have extra eggs I'll put them in cartons and refrigerate them to give to friends.

According to the USDA you can keep raw eggs in shell three to five weeks in the refrigerator. Do not freeze.

Roosters

The Story Of Dandy My Rooster

I was visiting my friend on her farm and she had her chickens running around free ranging. They all looked happy and healthy. Then I saw this tall skinny rooster penned up. He had really long funny looking legs that seemed to be two sizes too big for his skinny body. I asked her "what's up with that chicken" how come he is locked up all by himself? She said that he fights with her old, old rooster and she doesn't want Mr Skinny Long Legs to hurt the old man. She said that she has been trying to find him a new home because she feels bad keeping him locked up alone. I asked her if he does "the rooster dance". She looked at me with a puzzled expression, so I had to explain that a good rooster always does a rooster dance to signal the hen that he wants to breed and then the hen will squat down in cooperation. She said yes, she thinks he does. I said I will take him and see how he fits in on my Homestead.

She brought him over and I left him in the cage next to my hens so they could all get aquatinted. After a few days I just threw him in the coop. Nobody wanted anything to do with him. He seemed very happy to be in my big coop even though all the hens ran in the opposite direction every time he came near. My family all said "that sure is an ugly rooster" or "you picked an ugly rooster, why did you pick him?" I would answer back, he's not ugly and The response would be "look at those long legs." I would always defend him and say I like his long legs. That same conversation would take place every time my family came around and my response would always be the same, that I liked him and I liked his long legs.

Mr. Long Legs gets the name Dandy, because he is a Dandy of a rooster. I have to admit that I call him Dumdum like the lollipop. So now he has two names. Dandy boy slowly grew and grew into a huge poofy giant white rooster. Now his long legs are perfect, he just needed time to grow into them. He is the sweetest most patient rooster ever. He won all the hens over with his gentle charm, and now he is king of the castle.

A Run In With The Mule

One day I was in the barn feeding my "horses" - a mule, donkey, and draft pony. Charlie my mule was eating near the fence when Dandy decided to jump on Bubby my guinea hen and try and mate her.

She started to scream and squawk. Charlie struck the rooster off the guinea with his front hoof, then stomped his head into the sand with a second blow. I yelled at Charlie to stop while poor Dandy staggered away in fear. He went under my horse trailer and laid down.

I got a good look at him and didn't think he'd make it through the night. I decided not to touch him and just let him rest. I knew my farm dog would protect him so no predator would eat him over the night.

To my surprise and delight Dandy was still alive in the morning, and had moved a few feet and was now standing near my truck in the sunshine. I ever so gently picked him up, my huge poofy boy and carefully walked to my barn and sat him on the floor.

Of course I treated him like a king and put food and water in front of him. I could see only his head was hurt where Charlie stomped on it. The first stomp was on his back between his wings to knock him off Bubby. The second was meant to take him out. I wasn't mad at my mule Charlie because he thought Dandy was hurting Bubby and was protecting her. Mules and donkeys are very very protective. Dandy could only take a step or two, but he would not lay down during the day. I thought he is a fighter, he will make it. I put a pile of hay near him so he would be cozy at night.

He stayed in the barn for a few days then started to slowly walk to the coop where his hens were durning the day, but would come back to the barn at night. He looked sore, and stiff, but he walked to the coop to see his girls everyday. It took him months to heal. I'm sure his brain was swollen and we kept him quiet and babied him for months. I knew he was really on the mend when one night he jumped up onto the horse hitching rail to sleep.

Now he's blind in his right eye but seems healthy otherwise. He's a smart rooster and learned his lesson because I've never seen him try and breed that guinea again. He will do his rooster dance to her but when she doesn't squat down he moves on.

Dandy Becomes A Daddy

One of my oldest hens "Sweetie"started to sit on 6 eggs. I was so, so happy because I wanted some Dandy babies. The big mystery on the homestead was what color would the babies be. Mama is a black Australorp and of course Dandy is pure white.

Well, 21 days later I peeked in and saw a couple of white babies!!!!!! All of the babies were white like Dandy. Five out of the six eggs hatched but one baby was killed by another hen. That is very, very rare because a mother hen is fierce when protecting her chicks. I figured it's because she is an old, first time mama plus black Australorps are a super sweet,and gentle breed. Just to give her time to get the hang of things I put her and her babies in a huge tub in my barn. After the chicks grew I mover them all into the small pvc coop.

The Old Mother Hen Has Help

The chicks have a full time nanny. Bubby the guinea is the best most attentive nanny on the planet. She has made sure the chicky babies are safe at all times and is on duty 24/7.

It has been the cutest most joyful thing to watch the babies grow up with the two care takers hovering around at all times. I have to add I couldn't be happier that all four chicks are girls and will live here on my Homestead forever.

Do I Need A Rooster?

You don't need a rooster. Most neighborhoods don't even let you have one, because they are very noisy. Most people think that a rooster crows - Cock-a-doodle-doo - only at sunrise. But that's not true some crow all day every day.

Hens don't need a rooster to lay eggs. They'll lay just as many eggs without a rooster around. The eggs just won't be fertile, which means they'll never hatch into a baby. You can eat both fertile and infertile eggs and probably couldn't even tell the difference.

Even without a rooster your hens can get broody.

What Is Broody?

Broody is when a hen starts to sit on a pile of eggs with the goal of hatching them. Not all hens are broody, but a hen that is broody doesn't know the difference between fertile eggs and infertile eggs. Whether you have a rooster or not you can have a broody hen that wants to sit on a pile of eggs. For a broody hen it's instinctual, it's hard wired, you can not make her stop. What I do is collect the eggs every day so the hen doesn't get a big pile. If she sees a big pile of eggs she's more apt to try to sit on them and get broody.

How Do Chickens Reproduce?

When there's a rooster to fertilize the eggs, the hen is going to lay one egg in her nest every day. She's not going to sit on that one egg in her nest, she's going to get off and walk around and eat and whatever. The next day she's going to lay another egg in her nest box and leave the nest, go eat and act like normal. She's going to keep doing that until there's a pile of five or six eggs, whatever she decides. Then she's going to start sitting on those eggs.

She's not going to get off her nest, she's going to be on her nest 24/7. She's now in broody mode, she stays on her nest day and night and she's going to hatch her chicky babies!!! If there are several hens laying eggs in the same nest box the number of eggs grows quicker, which triggers her to be broody quicker. Even if they're not all her eggs, she will claim them, and sit on them and hatch them.

It takes 21 days for the baby chicks to hatch. Mama will get off her nest once in a while to get a bite to eat and get a drink. Once the chicks start to hatch it will take a few days for all the eggs to hatch, so give them time.

The broody hen will do this with or without a rooster. Meaning the eggs can be fertile and not fertile. The hen doesn't know the difference. So a lot of times you'll have a broody hen sitting on infertile eggs. The only way to prevent any issues is to just simply collect your eggs every day. If the hen has already decided to be broody and she's sitting on some eggs, I just gently push her off them and collect the eggs.

Picking A Good Rooster

If you live out in the country or your neighborhood allows rooster you might decide you want one. Here's what I've learned about picking a good rooster.

A good rooster will do "The Rooster Dance" - everyone needs to know what it is. Let me explain. When a good rooster wants to mate a hen, he will do a little rooster dance to signal her. The dance will make her squat down so they can breed. The rooster will put his wings out a little and flutter them as he walks around the hen. This signals her to squat down.

Over time and bad breeding the rooster dance has been bred out of a lot of roosters. what happens when the rooster doesn't do his mating dance is he will just grab the hen by the back of her head to start mating BUT the hen didn't get the signal so she thinks she is getting attacked and screams. The rooster gets frustrated and turns mean. Never keep a rooster that doesn't do the rooster dance and you shouldn't let it reproduce.

Chicken Coops

How To Build A Chicken Coop

PVC Chicken Tractor Plans

I love the design for this coop. You can use it as the permanent home for 2 hens. Or you can use it as the in between coop for baby chickens that need to grow bigger before you put them in the big coop. The best part is my design for this coop is really easy to build yourself in a weekend.

Shopping List

How many?	What?	Where to buy it?
11	3/4 Inch Schedule 40 PVC Pipes 10 Feet Long	Home Depot/Lowes/Hardware Store
8	3/4 Inch PVC Side Outlet Tee	Amazon
4	3/4 Inch PVC Tee	Home Depot/Lowes/Hardware Store
4	3/4 Inch Elbow (Standard)	Home Depot/Lowes/Hardware Store
10	3/4 Inch Elbow (Side Outlet)	Home Depot/Lowes/Hardware Store
1 Pack	11 Inch 75lb Strength Cable Ties (Pack of 100)	Amazon
1 Can	10oz Oatey Fusion Single Step PVC Cement	Home Depot/Lowes/Hardware Store
3 Cans	Spray Paint For Plastic	Amazon
1	1-1/4 Inch PVC Pipe Cutter	Amazon
1 Roll	Heavy Shade Sunblock Fabric	Amazon
1 Roll	Garden Zone 36x50 Green Vinyl 3x2 16-Gauge Garden Fence OR Galvanized Version (cheaper)	Amazon
1	Wooden 2x2	Home Depot/Lowes/Hardware Store

BeckysHomestead.com

Cut List

How many?	What?	What for?
33	32 Inches Long PVC Pipes	The main part of the frame and the door.
8	15 & 3/8s Inches Long PVC Pipes	The part that holds up the wooden 2x2.
1	36 Inches Long Wooden 2x2	The sleeping roost.

Tools List

How many?	What?	
1	Yard Stick	
1	PVC Pipe Cutter	
1	Sharpie Marker	
1	Wire Snips	
1	Drill with 3/8 Drill Bit for Wood	
1	Scissors	
1 pack	Rubber Gloves	

Step-by-Step Directions

Cut the pvc pipe into 33 pieces, each 32 inches long.

Use the leftovers to cut 8 more pieces, each 15 & 3/8s inches long.

Lay out the bottom with 4 side outlet elbows and 4 side outlet tees. Line everything up before you start gluing. Keep the openings lined up and the holes facing straight up.

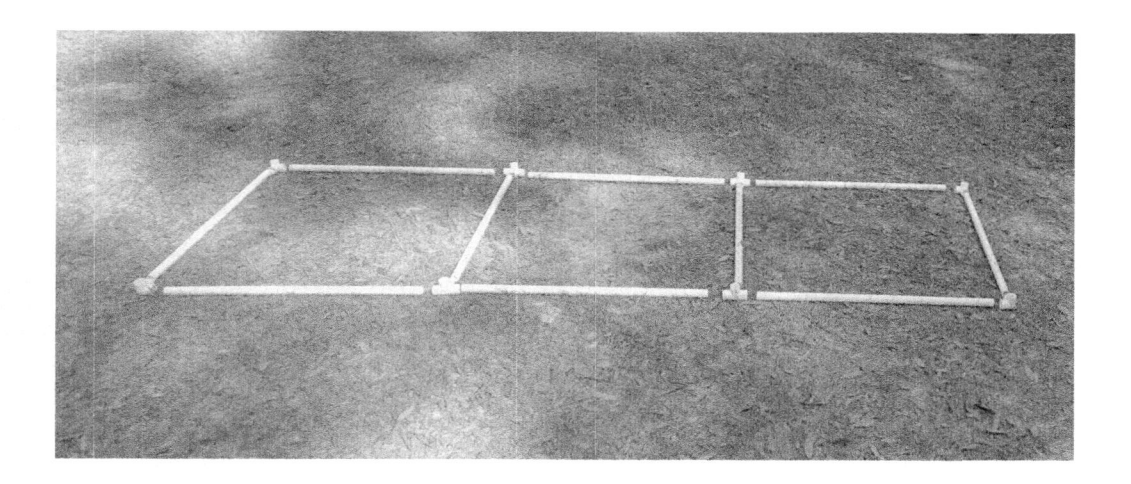

Dry fit the upright pieces. The side with the sleeping roost gets 4 of the 15 & 3/8s pieces, then 4 tees with the holes facing each other, then the last 4 of the 15 & 3/8s pieces. Dry fit everything and make sure it lines up before you start gluing.

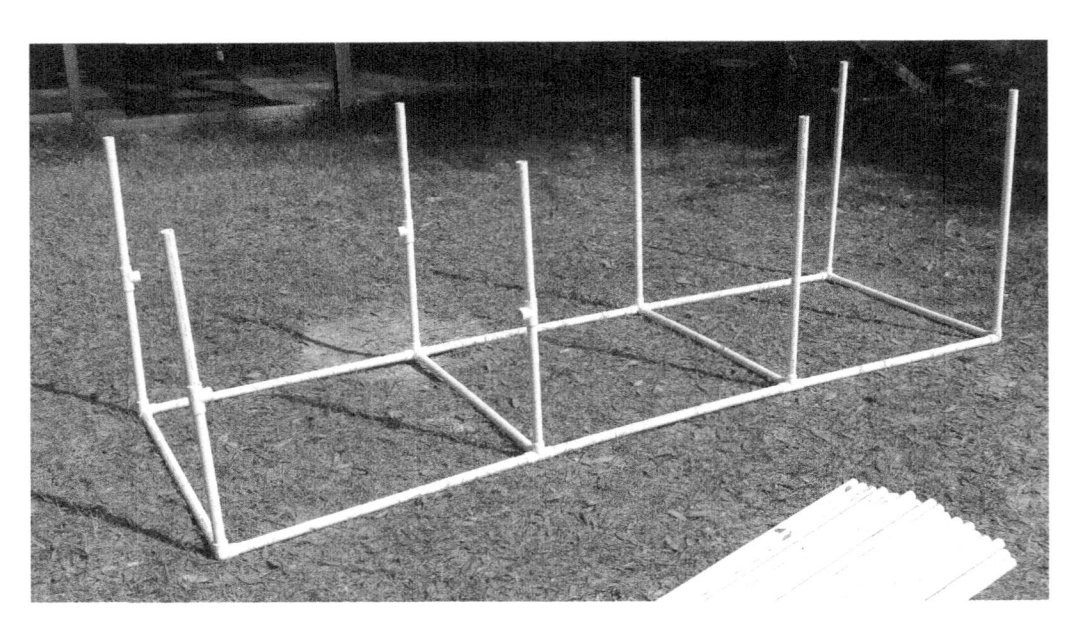

Glue in the upright pieces.

BeckysHomestead.com

81

Glue in the top pieces with the other 4 side outlet elbows and 4 side outlet tees.

The finished frame.

Glue together the door with the 4 normal elbows and 2 side outlet elbows.

Paint the frame with the spray paint. Save some paint for after you put on the wire because the wire will scratch some off and you can do some touchups after the wire is on.

Roll out the wire and lay the coop on its side on top of the wire. The side you start on will be where the door is.

Use the zip ties to attach the wire to the frame.

Flip the coop and keep attaching the wire to the 3 sides.

Leave a little extra wire when you cut the end so you can wrap it around the edge.

Roll out more wire and attach it to the door with zip ties.

Put wire on the roof. Leave a little extra wire past the opening so when the door in on there is an overlap.

Attach the door to the coop with loose zip ties.

Use the 3/8 drill bit to drill a hole on each end of the 36 inch wooden 2x2.

Put the wooden 2x2 across the pipes half way up the sides, and use zip ties through the holes to attach it to the frame. Get it really tight and secure because the chickens won't like it if it wiggles.

Wrap the coop in sun fabric and use the scissors to trim it. The zip ties will poke right through the sun fabric so it's easy to attach it to the coop.

Gotcha's To Avoid

Use tent stakes to stake down the coop to make it harder for the wind to blow it away, and harder for predators to lift up the edge and get inside.

Make sure you get schedule 40 PVC pipe. It's the thickest. The thin stuff is cheaper but it won't last.

If you make a mistake you can cut the pipe, fix it, then use a 3/4 coupling to put the pieces back together. PVC is easy to work with and very forgiving. Don't worry if you make a mistake when you glue the pipes together.

Cleaning Your Chicken Coop

Over time the inside of your chicken coop will get dusty, grow spider webs, and have piles of chicken poop under the sleeping roost. If you let this go your chickens will get mites, and they'll start getting sick.

That's why twice a year I clean my chicken coop. I start by raking out the old hay and chicken poop then I use a small power washer to spray everything clean.

Regularly cleaning your chicken coop is recommended for anyone who is looking to raise healthy backyard chickens. Here I provide you with some tips and tricks when it comes to cleaning the coop for your backyard chickens.

Change their water regularly

If one of your backyard chickens is unfortunate enough to contract an illness, this disease can quickly spread through your chickens shared water pan, Because of this, it is essential that you regularly change your chickens water supply! Not only will this stop diseases from spreading, but it will also stop the water from becoming stagnant and gross.

Rake up feathers;

Your chickens are going to molt their feathers all over the place, especially in the late fall when it starts to get colder. Soon, your chicken coop may have a new carpet of feathers.

Be sure to rake these feathers up regularly. When it comes to the floor of the coop, I love sand floors, sand drains good and chickens love to take a dust bath in the sand every day. Wood chips on the floor can be good if it's winter or you live in a colder climate

Pressure wash your coop whenever it needs a good cleaning.

Pressure washers are great for cleaning your chicken coop, and you should pressure wash your coop at least once every twelve months. By using water jets and a decent-quality soap, you can get rid of dirt and nasty bacteria easily! Pressure wash all the wood and be sure to keep an eye out for any mold or rotting wood – it's easy to do an inspection of the coop while cleaning it.

This way, you can make a note about anything that may need replacing or repairing soon. Feel free to pressure wash both the inside and the outside when cleaning your chicken coop, you want it to look nice and presentable!

next put down some Diatomaceous Earth.

After pressure washing, put down some high-quality, fresh water, food-grade Diatomaceous Earth. This will help to stop bugs such as lice and mites in their tracks, allowing your chickens to roam around without being bothered by pesky insects.

Weird Little Things Chickens Do And Why

Molting

There's a special time when chickens stop laying eggs and all their feathers fall out. That's because they're molting. Molting is when they lose they're old feathers and grow in new ones. Most chickens molt once a year and it's usually in the fall when the weather starts getting cooler. That seems like an odd time, like that's when they need their feathers the most, but something in the weather must trigger molting.

There will be a lot of feather in the coop, it can be worrisome the first time you see all the feathers on the ground and the hen looking like a hot mess, but in a couple months they will look better then ever. All healthy chickens molt. This is a good time to feed some extra animal protein. At this time I give them some extra meal worms, and the cat kibble. When the hen is done molting she'll look better than new and start laying eggs again.

Why Do My Chickens Pick Feathers And Eat Them?

I had a young Ameraucana hen with all her tail feathers pulled out. It was upsetting to see her with a featherless, irritated rear end. The other chickens where pecking her non stop, pulling out her tail feathers and eating them. I had to do something to stop it.

I learned feathers are mostly protein, if the chickens aren't getting enough animal protein in their diet they will start pecking each other and eating the feathers. If one of the hens is naturally more timid or skittish, the other hens will gang up on the weak one. Hens can be mean little birds if they aren't happy.

Once the weak hen has a red spot on her skin the other chickens just see meat and will peck it automatically thinking it's a bug or something. Remember, chickens have a pea brain. Thats why we have to take care if our little babies.

The first thing I did was take "Little Ms. No Tail Feathers" out of the big coop, and put her in the small pvc coop - the plans to build it are in this book. That way she could heal and grow her feathers back. Once her tail feathers fill all the way in I put her back in the big coop. The other hens leave her alone because the red spot tempting them to peck her is gone.

The other thing I did was make sure the chickens are getting enough animal protein in their diet. You can get higher protein chicken feed at the store, plus add meal worms to their diet.

I thought that since my chickens free range they're getting plenty of protein eating all the bugs, but what I learned is that there are only so many bugs in my yard so they weren't getting enough.

Plus late fall and winter all the bugs die or hide so I make sure to give them extra protein this time of year.

On a side note that's why chickens stop laying eggs when they're molting. It takes so much protein to grow new feathers that there's none left to make an egg.

Dust Bath

At times we see chickens doing strange little things and we think, what are they doing that for? One of those things is a dust bath. The chicken gets in the dirt or sand and turns on their side and flap their wings to cover their body with dirt. They want the dirt to make it's way all the way through their feathers to their skin. It is very important for chickens to have access to dirt or sand. Chickens start to dust bath very, very young and do it all their lives. The "dust" keeps their feathers healthy and may be a way to word off mites and lice.

If you keep your chickens in a coop full time because you work full time or have a lot of predators in your area, you can add a big pan of sand or dirt to the coop so they can do their thing. I find when you provide chickens with everything they need to be as close to natural as you can, and make sure not to over crowd, the chickens will be happy and healthy. A dust bath might seem like such a simple, silly little thing but your chickens really need and love it.

Ducks

What About Ducks?

Ducks are smart, strong and hardy compared to chickens. Ducks are awesome in a garden because ducks eat so many bugs without scratching up your plants, mulch and seedlings. A chicken can scratch up a garden and destroy all your hard work in a couple hours. I had that happen more than once.

Ducks hatch out more babies than most chicken. I notice it's because mama duck will collect up more eggs before she starts to set on them.

Baby ducks take longer to grow in the egg than chickens do. Ducks take twenty eight days to hatch.

It is important to know that daddy duck will soon try to kill his children. Once the babies can get around pretty good daddy will start to chase them away and be mean to them

Ducks need to be protected from prey animals at night so they need some kind of little pen to sleep in. My flip coop works really well for ducks.

Ducks eat pretty much what chickens eat, start with non medicated chick starter, then add crimped oats, and whole corn once they are bigger. Ducks can also eat some high quality cat kibble and meal worms.

Never ever put baby ducks in a tub of water and leave them. Their little ducky fuzz will get soaked through and they will sink and drowned. They will love a shallow pan of water to play in that they can just step out of.

Can ducks and chickens live together in the same coop?

I say no for two reasons. 1- ducks are bigger and stronger and will chase the chickens away from the food, and ducks will eat tons and tons of food with their shovel bills and get big and fat and poop like crazy. It's much better to keep them separate and dole out the duck food. 2- ducks need a small pool to take a dip in. Ducks breed in water so they need a little pool.

There are a lot of duck breeds. I like to be practical on my homestead so I like the ducks to have a job. Their job is working in the garden. Remember ducks eat bugs but don't scratch up the plants. Also I use their pool water as fertilizer for the garden. I want to say this again because it is so important, even though baby ducks can swim right away and mama will bring them into water, if you don't have the right setup where the babies can climb out easy they will drowned. That is because their baby fuzz gets saturated and they sink and drowned. It's really the feathers and oil on their feathers that keep ducks afloat for long hours. Ducks have an oil gland that they rub, and then spread it on their feathers.

Checklists

Baby Chickens Setup Checklist

Here's a list of the things you'll need to raise baby chicks until they're fully feathered and big enough to go in the coop.

- Large Tub
- Pine Shavings
- Shallow Water Dish - four inches deep for adults. one and a half inches deep for babies.
- Food Dish
- Unmedicated Chick Feed
- Chick Grit
- Thermometer or Temperature Regulator
- Heat Lamp
- Heat Bulb

Chicken Coop Checklist

This is what I put in my chicken coop.

- Hanging Feeder
- Water Tub
- Nest Boxes
- Sleeping Roost
- Grit

- Chicken Feed

Egg Laying Checklist

Chickens need everything just right to lay eggs. They're very sensitive birds. If one thing is off they won't lay eggs and you'll be scratching your head wondering why. Here's a list of things you can check if they aren't laying eggs:

- The coop and nest boxes can't be near any busy traffic or noise. Is the road near their coop with cars going past? Are there kids or pets running past their coop?

- Is there anything shiny reflecting into the coop? A chrome bumper or white vinyl siding can reflect a lot of light and heat that will stress out the hens.

- Are they getting enough calcium? They need crushed oyster shell grit to digest their food and get enough calcium.

- Are they getting enough protein? They need animal protein from free range bug catching, or from food you give them like bagged meal worms and high protein feed.

- Are they laying their eggs someone else and not in the coop? They might be laying eggs just fine, but they're hidden somewhere else and not in the coop. If that is going on, you will have to lock them in the coop for ten days to get them back on track laying in their nest box.

Chicken Breed Index

Australorp

History

The Australorp was introduced as a dual purpose breed in the nineteen twenties. They achieved worldwide fame after breaking several world records for laying eggs. Since then it has been a well-known breed in the western world.

It's 1 of eight poultry breeds developed in Australia and accepted by the Australian Poultry Standard. Black is the most common color of the breed and it's the only recognized color in the United States of America.

Personality

The black Australorp's feathers have a greenish purple shimmer in the sunlight. This gives the feathers a beautiful iridescence.

They're happy in the coop, but they love free ranging to look for bugs. Overall, Australorp chickens love to stay active, so make sure your coop is plenty big enough and never over crowd. They're fast-growing birds with a shy personality, but as soon as they settle in, they'll follow you around so you can give them treats!

Health and Care

Australorps are a healthy and robust heritage breed. So there isn't any special attention needed. They have a life expectancy of about ten years.

In terms of care, Australorps don't need any additional grooming techniques apart from what normal chickens require. The breed is on the heavy side, so they can't go far and they aren't flighty. So you don't need to trim their wing feathers.

They don't have any particular diseases specific to their breed. But they should be dewormed regularly. Vaccination may be necessary if there are known bird diseases in your area. Otherwise, your chicken will stay healthy as long as you protect them from predators.

Egg Laying Ability

Australorps will get broody occasionally. but don't expect it too often.

Australorps are great egg layers. They will definitely satisfy your cravings for omelets! They lay about two hundred and fifty to three hundred large light brown eggs yearly. This is great news for all you egg enthusiasts!

Color Variations

Australorps come in three different variations. This includes the following:

White

Black

Blue

But the white Australorp isn't popular.

Appearance

Australorps are big birds weighing about six to eight pounds. They're soft and beautiful feathers, are great to look at under the sunlight, because their feathers look bright and vibrant with subtle colors of green and purple.

Australorps can endure cold winter and hot temperatures with ease. They can lay eggs during extreme cold and hot temperatures

Ameraucana

History

The history of this breed dates back to the 1920s. It originated from two types of chickens from the Mapuche Indians – the Collonca and Quetero.

It's unclear whether both breeds were bred together naturally or by human intervention.

This new breed eventually became the Araucana chicken in Chile. When it was brought to America and domesticated it became known as the "Ameraucana" – a combination of the words "American" and "Araucana."

The Ameraucana and the original breed, Araucana, according to the APA (American Poultry Association), are considered purebred blue-egg breeds.

Appearance

1. These chickens are docile and have a skittish nature
2. This breed is smaller in size, compared to other chickens.
3. They weigh six pounds to seven pounds
4. The Ameraucana chicken comes in different colors. Some of them are: black, blue, brown, silver, white, red and blue wheaten
5. They carry their tails upright at 45 degrees to their body
6. They have eyes that are reddish bay in color
7. Roosters are known for their aggressiveness

Egg Laying Ability

Known for light blue eggs, Ameraucanas produce three to four medium sized eggs per week. They sometimes lay greenish eggs.

This breed is best suited for egg production.

Bantam Chickens

History

A bantam chicken is a small version of a normal chicken. The bantams vary from two thirds to one half the size of normal birds. The name 'Bantam' came from the Bantan's seaport in Indonesia.

When sailors stopped by the port looking for clean water and fresh food, they were awed by the local chickens. These chickens were smaller compared to the breeds back home. The word, Bantan was changed to Bantam in English. As a result, small chickens were called bantams.

Personality

In general Bantams have a sweet character and are friendly to other chickens and humans. Some might get aggressive, particularly during mating season. Overall Bantam chickens have unique and lovely personalities.

Normal size chickens are heavy, so the bantam's small size makes it great for kids to handle and pet.

Health and Care

Just like regular chickens Bantams need a strong and safe coop to call home. Make sure your little bantams are protected from dangerous predators lurking around.

Egg Laying Ability

The egg laying ability of a bantam chicken depends on the breed you get, but you can expect about four to five eggs weekly.

Bantams have a life span of four to eight years, depending on the type of bantam.

Egg Size

Since a bantam hen is quite a bit smaller than a standard chicken her eggs will be smaller.

If you want to use bantam eggs for baking purposes, you may wonder how many bantam eggs equals one standard chicken egg. It depends on the egg's size, but in general two bantam eggs equals one standard egg, while three bantam eggs equal two standard eggs.

Barred Rock

History

In 1869, the Barred rock chicken was first created as a breed in England after crossbreeding Black Javas, Cochin, Dominiques and other chicken breeds such as the Dorkings and Malay. Also called "rocks" in breeder circles, the Barred rock chicken is the ideal strong breed for winter weather.

For many years, the barred rock chicken was the most bred in the US. While the barred rock is known as just one unique breed, crossbreeding has produced a lot of similar breeds under Plymouth Rock.

Health and Care

Barred rocks can adapt to many conditions, that's why they're called hardy birds. They adapt very well to most weather so they're the perfect breed for small farm owners. Of corse always keep their coop clean and change their water frequently.

Appearance

Barred rocks come in different colors; black, barred, white, buff, blue, silver, penciled, Columbian, and partridge.

The "barred" coloring is quite popular, hence the name Barred Rock.

So a Barred Rock chicken is a white-and-black Plymouth Rock chicken. It's proper breed name is Barred Plymouth Rock.

Personality

Since eighteen seventy four this breed has been considered a heritage breed.

Barred Rocks are know for being calm toward people which makes them great for kids. They like being handled and love the care and attention.

While a lot of people recognize Barred Rocks for producing eggs, their personality and disposition make them a family-friendly breed for backyard chickens. I find them to be people friendly but mean to other chickens.

Egg Laying Ability

Barred rocks are year-round layers if you feed them right. Producing four big brown eggs weekly. Expect this chicken to start laying eggs at about sixteen to twenty weeks old.

Brahma

History

The Brahma is a big chicken breed introduced in the US from large birds. The birds were brought in from Shanghai in the eighteen fifties to nineteen thirty.

What gave the Brahma its peculiar characteristics was cross-breeding it with the Bangladesh Chittagong chickens.

The features include a pea comb which differentiates it from the Cochin.

In December 1852, the Brahmas were first transported to England, when George Burnham sent 9 "Gray Shanghaes" as a gift to Queen Victoria. The Dark Brahma was created by English breeders from the Gray Shanghaes and then re-exported to the US.

Personality

Brahma chickens are docile giants with feathered feet, legs, and fluffy feathering. They're known as meat birds, but the hens lay eggs regularly and are excellent mothers when they hatch chicks. Brahmas also make good pets because of their tame and quiet nature. They tolerate and enjoy being held and petted.

Even though they like confinement, they are great foragers. They are the perfect breed for cold weather, thanks to their thick feathering. Avoid wet, muddy swampy areas since it may cause foot problems. You have to make sure you keep their coop super dry by dumping bags of sand in their coop. Sand drains well and they will love to take a dust bath in it once it warms up. Although Brahmas aren't overly broody, some will set on eggs.

Care and Health

Brahmas can stay in a three foot tall coop as their huge size prevents them from flying. Also, they love dry conditions because they have foot feathers. If you let Brahmas walk around in the moist soil, they'll develop mud balls. If these mud balls stay on their feet too long, they may lose the tip of their toes or lose their nails. With the right care, they will thrive in a warmer and colder climate.

Brahmas need a lot of cool, fresh water with electrolytes daily. Also, they need shade, dust baths, and good ventilation. Even though Brahmas are slow moving, they like to walk around and free range and it is good exercise for them.

Egg Laying Ability

Brahmas lay three big light brown eggs per week on average.

Appearance

On average a mature Brahma rooster weighs about 12 pounds!

The hens weigh approximately 9 pounds.

They have dense plumage, with feathers on their legs and their middle toes.

Color Variations

Brahmas have 5 recognized color variations; dark, light, black, buff and white, but the white and black are seldom found.

Cochin

History

The Cochins first came into existence in the 1840s. The breed was formerly called 'Cochins-China'. In actuality, Cochins were imported from Vietnam. The first imported Cochins do not look like the Cochins of today.

Captain Edward Belcher gave the first Cochins to Queen Victoria. During that period, 'hen fever' took over the United States and the UK. The hen fever led to the development of the Cochin and the Brahma chickens. At the time these birds could be sold and bought for a lot of money!

The first Cochins were excellent layers. But the moment poultry enthusiasts began to "mess" with the breed the Cochins suffered. They looked gorgeous, but the meat became awful tasting and they lay fewer eggs.

Personality

Cochins are friendly and calm chickens, even the Cochins roosters are friendly. They rarely get mean or aggressive. The hens may get broody and are excellent mothers if they do. Cochins will sit on any fertile eggs you give them.

They're used as foster mothers for deserted chicks. But it depends on the type of Cochin and whether she is ready to go broody or not. You can contain Cochins easily since they are not great flyers.

They tolerate confinement well, because they are quite big and lazy.

Appearance

The Cochin chicken breeds are large sized, weighing about 10 pounds. Also, Cochins have plumage over their feet and head with a single comb.

Health and Care

One major health concern is obesity. Cochins are lazy and mellow chickens. They don't forage a lot, making them prone to leg injuries. Don't over feed them, they do not need a feeder twenty four, seven. This breed only needs to be feed in the morning and once in the evening.

So make sure you keep an eye on their food intake and adjust it if they are getting too fat.

Just like other fluffy hens, check for parasites like mites and lice regularly. Other than these issues, Cochins are a healthy breed and can live for about 10 years.

Egg Laying Ability

Cochins lay big light brown eggs, they can go broody several times a year.

They can lay about 180 to 200 eggs a year. Cochins prefer to lay during the winter months just like the Brahma chicken.

Easter Egger

History

An Easter Egger chicken is any breed that has the "blue egg" gene. Easter Eggers don't meet the breed standard stated in the American Bantam Association's standards or the American Poultry Association's standard. As a result, most hatcheries have unknowingly named their Easter Eggers Araucanas or Ameraucanas. The Araucana, Easter Eggers, and Ameraucana came from the same stock, which spread from the Falklands and Chile.

A lot of breeds were involved in making the Easter Eggers. No wonder they come in unique patterns and colors. Oocyanin, a pigment that's deposited on the shell surface accounts for the green and blue color.

Personality

Easter Eggers are docile, and friendly birds. So they're an ideal choice for your family and backyard flock. If you care for Easter Eggers when they're young, this calm breed will be kid-friendly. They'll follow you around whenever you let them out to free range.

Characteristics

Easter Egger chickens are related to the Araucana and Ameraucana breeds, but they are a mix of various breeds. As a result, they don't fit either the Araucana or the Ameraucana breed standards. Their eggs differ widely in conformation and color. Normally they have muffs and pea combs, but come in unique colors.

Even though every Easter Egger has unique characteristics they all tend to be smaller and can lay pink, green, or blue colored eggs. Easter Egger roosters weigh about 5 lbs, while hens weigh approximately 4 lbs.

Care and Health

You can keep Easter Eggers in your backyard coop. They are hearty and tolerant to warm or cold temperatures. You don't need to heat the coop because they won't develop the ability to endure the cold.

Easter Eggers are active birds. They love foraging and roaming, so make sure they have a huge run in their coop to keep them happy and healthy. If you don't have enough space, you can get bantam Easter Eggers. they are just like the normal Easter Eggers, but a smaller size.

Egg Laying Ability

Eggs laid by Easter Eggers vary in color greatly. Some Easter Eggers may lay turquoise, sky blue, or teal eggs. Also, others can lay pea green, sage green, hues of pink!! Each chicken only lays 1 color egg, so if you want different color shades, plan on having several hens.

Easter Eggers start laying eggs at about seven months old, which is later than other chickens. But once they start, they are excellent layers.

Orpington Chickens

History

In the late 1800s, the Orpington was first introduced in Great Britain. This breed was created by William Cook, a coachman who resided in Orpington, Kent. The breed was developed by crossbreeding a Black Plymouth Rock and a Minorca.

The primary colors can be white, black, buff, splash, and blue. But the Buffs are the most common.

Personality

Orpington have big poofy loose feathers. They look bigger than they are, because of all those feathers which makes them cold hardy birds, but of corse every chicken needs a good coop to be happy and healthy.

Orpingtons can be friendly and docile. The buffs are calm – the only time you'll see them run is for food.

They love attention and are good with kids. Orpingtons lay big light brown eggs

Health and Care

They love to free range during the day, and roost in their sturdy coop at night.

The coop can a proper chicken shed or an old shed, which needs one nesting box for every six to eight hens.

Keep the door of the coop open during the day. Doing this will make it easy for them to return to lay their eggs in their nest box.

Orpington Varieties

Orpingtons have a few varieties aside from Buff, but these color variations are difficult to find.

Lavender Orpington

This is a very big docile bird and is a great breed to keep. Also, they are great with kids. Lavender Orpingtons are good at laying eggs, producing 175 to 200 big brown eggs yearly. A lot of Lavender Orpington chickens can go broody and hatch their chicks.

Splash Orpington

This variety is nearly all white with blue and black splashes on its body. A healthy Splash Orpington hen will lay 120 to 200 eggs yearly and weigh between seven to ten pounds. A rooster can weigh even more.

Buff Orpington

The Buff Orpington is a docile bird and quite easy to handle. They lay light brown eggs. While buff owners can tame them with ease, this breed

doesn't lay as many eggs as some breeds, but looking at those big beautiful poofy feathers makes up for it.

Black Orpington

The Black Orpington is the oldest color and it's traced back to 1886 when William Cook decided to form a new utility chicken. This breed can lay about two hundred eggs yearly and can weigh between eight and ten pounds.

Blue Orpington

This breed is affectionate, quiet, and calm like the Buff Orpington. The blue hens lay about two hundred eggs a year. The eggs have a light brown tint.

White Orpington

The White Orpingtons are raised for their temperament and looks. The hen can lay about two hundred eggs yearly. The hens can weigh up to ten pounds, and roosters can weigh up twelve pounds.

Buff Orpington

History

In the 1800s, a lot of people were interested in new chicken breeds. Back then it was called "Hen Fever". Everyone wanted American chicken breeds with dual purposes.

Many new breeds were developed in England and the Buff Orpington was one of them. Orpington chickens became popular in England and they were exported to other countries.

Personality

Buff Orpingtons have unique personalities. They like to go for patrols and walk in the yard. They love being carried, held, and scratched. Some buffs will sit on your legs while you read a newspaper or a book.

They'll never peck at you except when they want your attention. Buff Orpington roosters are gentle, with some even displaying friendly personalities. As a result buffs are a popular homestead favorite. Plus, they make great broody mothers for young chicks.

Appearance

Buffs have big fluffy feathers. Most times, they're called the "Big Buffs," as they're loosely feathered which makes them look heavier than their actual weight.

Health and Care

Buffs are large special birds that make excellent egg layers and family members. Just like any bird, caring for Buff Orpingtons involves good housing and proper nutrition to ensure your bird is strong, healthy, and productive.

During winter, Buff Orpingtons will need a heat source, particularly when the weather is extremely cold. They'll also need bedding to keep them warm and healthy.

Egg Laying Ability

Buffs are a dual-purpose chicken, so they're bred for both eggs and meat. Also, they're known as heavy birds due to their big size at maturity.

Roosters can weigh about 10 pounds, while hens can weigh about eight pounds. Since Buffs are large birds, they need enough outdoor space and big coops to stretch their legs.

Buff Orpingtons can be good layers. They lay nice brown eggs. They can lay two hundred up to two hundred and eighty eggs yearly. If you are raising buffs as meat birds, they'll be ready at about 22 weeks. In general, they're often considered the ideal dual-purpose chicken.

Plymouth Rock

History

Introduced in the 1900s the Plymouth Rock is among the most common breeds in the US. The breed was named after the city of Plymouth, and rose in popularity in America due to its great egg-laying abilities.

In the 1950s it was crossed with several breeds when commercial chicken production and factory farming became prevalent. As a result, purebred Plymouths became difficult to find.

Temperament and Personality

The Plymouth Rock has a tame-able and sweet temperament. It's a great addition to backyard flocks.

Since they feel relaxed around humans, they love being dotted on and pet. They have strong maternal senses, so they're perfect for brooding.

Plymouth Rocks are strong in cold temperatures. So they're the ideal choice in cold regions.

They need a good coop in dark shade to protect them from hot weather and bright sunlight. every chicken needs a little sun every day, but shade is much more important with animals living outside.

Appearance

Plymouth Rocks are a heavy and sturdy breed. Their beaks and legs are yellow in color, while their combs and lobes are red. They have loose feathers. Plymouth Rocks come in many different beautiful colors.

The recognized variations include; white, barred, and buff. Other variations include buff-Columbian, blue laced, Columbian, and silver partridge.

Health

Plymouth Rock's aren't prone to any serious health conditions. Feeding crushed garlic and apple cider vinegar once or twice a year can help bolster all chickens immune system.

Plymouth Rocks can be susceptible to overheating or frostbite if the weather hits extremes.

Care

Plymouth Rocks are fairly standard in terms of maintenance, diet and grooming, no wonder they're a favorite breed for a lot of chicken owners. It doesn't matter if you're experienced or just starting out in backyard poultry!

Check for lice, worms, and parasites regularly.

Provide a coop strong and comfortable enough for each bird in the flock.

Make sure to place chickens with similar characters together. I find Barred Rocks to be bullies to other chickens and they are strong, so they can really hurt other chickens when they start to pick on them. Keep your eye on them to make sure every one is getting alone.

Egg Laying Abilities

They are productive egg layers. They'll keep laying all through the winter, when other birds would stop laying or reduce the number of eggs they produce. Expect Plymouth Rocks to lay over two hundred brown eggs yearly. Their eggs are large in size, perfect for egg enthusiasts or omelet lovers.

Silkie Chickens

History

Silkie chickens are one of the most well-known breeds. With their loving personalities and eccentric characteristics, they're the most preferred breed to keep as pets.

It's believed that Silkie Chickens come from Asia. The first records of Silkie existence were in the 13th century when Marco Polo wrote about Silkies on his way to China. He stated that these fluffy birds had the hair of cats and dark skin.

Once this breed became popular in the West, different myths were written about them.

Personality

This breed has eccentric personalities. They're reserved and calm, but can make a loud noise when laying an egg or sounding a predator alarm.

Silkies make great pets. They don't fly high, so you can keep them in the backyard easily. They're great with kids and love being held and fawned over.

Broodiness

Silkies are known for their desire to brood and hatch chicks. Also, Silkie will hatch chickie babies many times in a one season. They can spend months sitting on one brood after another, waiting for them to hatch. Silkies makes caring and wonderful mothers. They can also adopt ducks, turkeys, quail, and other birds as their own.

Caring For Silkies

Thanks to their docile behavior and fluffy feathers, silkies makes a great starter bird for those looking to start a backyard flock. This a perfect breed for people who don't have a lot of room or who don't want big chickens. If you keep them healthy, clean, and safe, they'll live for up to seven years.

How To Care For Silkies

Prepare a coop with four square feet for each bird in the flock.

Build a wooden hen house that predators can't break into at night.

Place chickens with similar personalities together.

Feed silkies twice a day and make sure they have plenty of clean water.

Trim silkie feathers around their rear and face when needed.

You can vaccinate silkies to prevent Marek's disease.

Egg Laying Abilities

Silkies lay approximately one hundred to one hundred and fifty eggs yearly on average. It's safe to say that they're not the best egg layers in the world. This is due to the fact that silkies brood frequently. Chickens don't lay eggs while brooding or raising chicks. Also, egg-laying capabilities in Silkies depend on the bird. Some silkies lay daily all through the year, while some lay weekly, but their cuteness more than makes up for their lack of eggs. If you don't have a rooster, make sure you collect the eggs every day so the hen doesn't go broody.

Wyandotte

History

The Wyandotte chicken was introduced in the US in the 1870s by John Ray, H. M. Doubleday, Fred Houdlette, and L. Whittaker

The silver-laced was the first Wyandotte chicken. In 1883, it was added to the American Standard of Perfection. Also, it was taken to Britain in 1883. While the origin of the Wyandotte chicken remains a mystery, the dark Brahmas and silver spangled Hamburgs are important breeds. They were involved in the first crosses in creating the Wyandotte.

Personality

The Wyandottes are big and gorgeous divas. They walk around the yard, displaying their beautiful colors and shun any bird that crosses their path. Wyandottes are docile, but will confront anyone who threatens their pecking order. Clearly, their at the top the pecking order.

Wyandotte are gentle and calm birds. Most of them are great mothers. Compared to some other breeds Wyandottes are pretty broody . So, if you want to hatch out chicky babies a Wyandotte might just be the breed for you!

Size

Wyandotte chickens are a dual purpose breed. They are good for different purposes. They can serve as meat birds and are good layers too. A matured Wyandotte hen will weigh about six pounds, and roosters weigh around nine pounds.

Care

Generally, Wyandottes are self-sufficient birds. Their fluffy butts can be an issue because their poo can stick to their butt feathers, to avoid this problem, just trim their butt feathers occasionally.

Health Issues

Wyandotte chickens don't have any health issues. Frequent deworming for preventing internal parasites, and make sure they have crushed oyster shells at all times along with

Nutritious feed and clean water. All chickens need a big safe chicken coop.

Egg Laying Ability

Wyandotte chickens lay big brown eggs. They're great layers, laying about two hundred big brown eggs yearly. They can lay eggs all through the summer and winter months. While other breeds stop laying eggs during extreme weather conditions.

Hatching

A Wyandotte hen has a strong broody instinct. What's more, they are great mothers as they tend to their new chicks with ease, love, and care.

Wyandotte Chicken Variations:

Gold Laced

Patridge

Silver Laced

Blue laced

White

Blue

Columbian

Black

Penciled

Buff

Appearance

Wyandottes have rich coloring with a lacing of the second color on every feather. They're fluffy with thick yellow featherless legs. They also have a rose comb and small wattles close to the face.

Silver Laced Wyandotte

History

The Silver Laced Wyandotte was the first American chicken developed with a dual purpose in mind. While it's origin isn't known, genetic material from the silver spangled Hamburgs and dark Brahmas were possible contributors. Other likely breeds to the genetic pool were Polish and Breda fowl.

Personality

Silver Laced Wyandottes are known for their waddles, bright red combs, and stunning white and black feathers. Their comb is called the rose comb, flat and no spikes. Wyandottes have a good temperament, but some varieties have strong personalities making them look unfriendly.

Though the Silver Laced Wyandotte chickens are friendly chickens, they aren't 'cuddly. Also, they can be talkative, but it varies from chicken to chicken.

They're usually dominant over other chickens. So this breed is at the top of the pecking order. They don't harass other chickens, but seldom bullied.

Appearance

Silver Laced Wyandotte chickens are colorful painted birds. They look stunning all dressed up in their beautiful white and black lacy feathers.

They are stunning chickens and medium-sized when they are fully grown. The hens weigh about six pounds, while roosters weigh about nine pounds.

Health and Care

Silver Laced Wyandotte chickens are robust in health and in appearance as well. No specific diseases have been recorded for the Silver Laced Wyandottes. Any breed with thick feathering has to be watched for lice or mites. If you see them, catch the chicken and dust with diatomaceous earth every day for seven days in a row. clean the coop and sprinkle with DE once a week for a month Also, you may need to trim the rear end feathers one in a while.

Egg Laying Ability

This breed will start laying eggs when they are about twenty four to twenty eight weeks old. A Silver Laced Wyandotte hen will lay about two hundred nice eggs a year. The eggs are brownish in color and medium-sized. The eggs are a bit smaller, but they're still a strong dual purpose chicken.

Made in the USA
Coppell, TX
25 April 2022